MAY - - 2009

W9-AST-002

DISCARD

COSTUME AROUND THE WORLD
France

Kathy Elgin

CHELSEA CLUB HOUSE

An Imprint of Chelsea House Publishers

Produced for Chelsea Clubhouse by Bailey Publishing Associates Ltd
11a Woodlands, Hove BN3 6TJ
England

Project Manager: Roberta Bailey
Editor: Alex Woolf
Text Designer: Jane Hawkins
Picture Research: Roberta Bailey and Shelley Noronha

Chelsea Clubhouse
An imprint of Chelse House Publishers
132 West 31st Street
New York NY 10001

ISBN 978-0-7910-9766-3

Library of Congress Cataloging-in-Publication Data
Costume around the world.—1st ed.
     v. cm.
   Includes bibliographical references and index.
   Contents: [1] China / Anne Rooney—[2] France / Kathy Elgin—[3] Germany / Cath Senker—[4] India / Kathy Elgin—[5] Italy / Kathy Elgin—[6] Japan / Jane Bingham—[7] Mexico / Jane Bingham—[8] Saudi Arabia / Cath Senker—[9] Spain / Kathy Elgin—[10] United States / Liz Gogerly.
   ISBN 978-0-7910-9765-6 (v. 1)—ISBN 978-0-7910-9766-3 (v. 2)—ISBN 978-0-7910-9767-0 (v. 3)—ISBN 978-0-7910-9768-7 (v. 4)—ISBN 978-0-7910-9769-4 (v. 5)—ISBN 978-0-7910-9770-0 (v. 6)—ISBN 978-0-7910-9771-7 (v. 7)—ISBN 978-0-7910-9773-1 (v. 8)— ISBN 978-0-7910-9772-4 (v. 9)—ISBN 978-0-7910-9774-8 (v. 10) 1. Clothing and dress—Juvenile literature.
   GT518.C67 2008
   391—dc22   2007042756

Chelsea Clubhouse books are available at special discounts when purchased in bulk quantities for businesses, associations, institutions, or sales promotions. Please call our Special Sales Department in New York at (212) 967-8800 or (800) 322-8755.

You can find Chelsea Clubhouse on the World Wide Web at: http://www.chelseahouse.com

Printed and bound in Hong Kong

10 9 8 7 6 5 4 3 2 1

The publishers would like to thank the following for permission to reproduce their pictures:
Bailey Publishing Associates Ltd: 28.
Chris Fairclough Worldwide Ltd: 22, 23, 27.
Corbis: 11, 16 (Atlantide Phototravel), 26 (James Russell).
Jupiter Images: 13 (bottom), 19.
Rex Features: 8 (Patrick Frilet), 10 (Sipa Press), 13 top (Sipa Press), 14 and title page (Travel Library), 15 (Patrick Frilet), 17 (Paul Cooper), 18, 24 (Kabacsil/Phanie), 29 (Sipa Press).
Topfoto: 4, 5 (Roger-Viollet), 6, 7, 9, 20, 21 (Image Works), 25.

Contents

A Rich Heritage

France is the largest country in Western Europe and has a rich cultural heritage. It gets its name from a people called the Franks, who settled there in the fifth century. Before that it was part of the Roman Empire. France has always been a wealthy country with a high standard of living. This has allowed the arts to flourish and the French people to enjoy good food and wine and fine clothes.

The textile industry
Textiles and clothing have always been an important part of the French economy. In the 15th century, northern France was the center of the wool trade. Merchants imported high-quality wool from England to be spun and woven into cloth, and workers in these trades became highly skilled.

In this 15th-century cloth workshop, dyers are coloring the woolen cloth in a wooden vat.

4

On this poster for an international exhibition, France is represented by the figure of Marianne, on the left.

French workmanship became famous all over Europe and eventually developed into today's fashion industry.

The face of France

Marianne, the national emblem of France, appears on stamps, coins, and other official documents. Marianne's Greek-style robes and Phrygian cap (a symbol of freedom) are a reminder of the French Revolution of 1789. Many famous actresses, including Brigitte Bardot and Catherine Deneuve, have been the model for Marianne.

Roots

These days, young French people wear the same clothes as people their age in America. However, the French are very patriotic and are proud that each of France's 22 regions still has its own distinctive food, culture, and costume. Although three-quarters of the population live in towns and cities, French people still value traditional rural life. Even those who move to another part of the country remain attached to the place where they were born. Although hardly anyone wears regional costume every day, many people have an outfit for special occasions.

Revolutionary Trends

Whatever the period, France was always at the forefront of fashion. The medieval courts of the dukes of Burgundy set the fashion throughout Europe for what noblemen and noblewomen should wear.

Beautifully illustrated books of the period show elegant, rich people relaxing in fur-trimmed silk and velvet. Meanwhile in the background, peasants work in simple wool smocks and stockings. Women wore long, flowing robes, but men showed off their shapely legs with short tunics and colored stockings.

Frills and farthingales
The fashion trend for women in the 16th century was the French farthingale, a wired petticoat that made the skirt stand out far from the waist. By the late

The finely dressed nobleman in this lovely Book of Hours is probably the person who commissioned it. Artists usually flattered their patron by putting him in the picture.

17th century, low-necked gowns used huge amounts of fabric, either silk or cotton. Men wore knee-length fitted coats and knee breeches made of silk and rich brocades with high-heeled shoes. Frills and lace were very popular for both sexes.

Fashion and folly

Fashion reached the height of excess during the reign of Louis XVI (1774–1791). It became a symbol of the inequality of society and fed the climate of unrest that led to the French Revolution in 1789. By the end of the 18th century, Paris was established as the fashion capital of Europe and the first fashion magazines were being published.

By the early 19th century, when Napoleon was in power, fashion went to the other extreme. The simple, draped styles of ancient Greece, known as "Empire style," were popular in fine cotton and muslin, trimmed with ribbons.

The Empire style gave women an elegant simplicity, but many tried to make the necklines more revealing.

Looking rich and looking poor

During the French Revolution, aristocrats were hunted down. Hoping to avoid execution, they abandoned their finery and wore working-class clothes. It became the fashion to look poor. Revolutionaries wore a red, white, and blue cockade on their hats. Anyone not wearing one was immediately suspected of not being loyal to the revolution.

Land of Valley and Vine

The French landscape varies from snow-covered mountains to flat, lush farmland, acres of vineyards, and deep river valleys. Inland, farmers grow wheat or keep livestock in order to produce France's astonishing variety of cheeses. The typical costume of farmworkers everywhere is a cotton shirt, usually blue or checked, and loose pants.

In summer, shepherds still move their flocks up to pastures in the high mountains, as indicated by this traditional roadside sign.

In the mountains

Southern France is dominated by dramatic mountain ranges. The Alps separate France from Switzerland and Italy, and the Pyrenees form the border with Spain. Skiing and snow sports are major attractions here, and a whole industry of outdoor clothing has grown up around them.

The windy north

The area north of Paris is flat and windy. Because of the cool climate and abundance of native sheep, people in this area traditionally wore wool clothing. A typical outfit included several layers of shirts, a vest, and a jacket for men and a dress and shawl for women, plus hats and caps. The area became heavily industrialized in the 19th century and was one of the first to lose its traditional culture.

Between two seas

France is bordered on two sides by the sea, which encouraged the growth of very different fishing communities. In Brittany, with its rugged coastline and stormy weather, the local fishermen and sailors traditionally wore striped sweaters and jackets made of thick sailcloth. On the southeast coast, which has a mild, Mediterranean climate, local fisherwomen were famous for their cotton skirts and blouses.

Swapping styles

The French regions of Alsace and Lorraine border Germany. After various wars, they became part of one country, then the other. Each time, the people had to change their whole culture, even their language. This was reflected in the style of clothing, which was often more German than French.

Breton sailors are proud to show off their traditional costumes at the many folk festivals that now take place all over the region.

Holy Days and Holidays

Although there is no state religion in France, over half of the population is Catholic and the Church continues to influence cultural life. Christian holidays and festivals are celebrated throughout the country. Statues from the local church are carried in processions through the streets, and everyone puts on his or her best clothes to watch.

The banners used in church processions are the community's most prized possessions.

The festival of Corpus Christi is celebrated all over France. Priests, wearing their most elaborate embroidered vestments and followed by the choir, carry the church's communion cup around the parish. They walk beneath gold-embroidered canopies, and the streets are often covered with rose petals. Little girls wear new white dresses and carry flowers.

Day of the Kings

Another opportunity for dressing up is the Day of the Kings, on January 6. Children in long robes and gold paper crowns pretend to be the Three Kings. They go from door to door, begging for food

Children in this Corpus Christi procession wear flower headdresses and carry baskets of flowers and sweets.

for the poor. Although many French do not attend church regularly, they have made a big effort to retain or revive these traditions.

Religion in schools

Recently, religious clothing has become an issue in France. By law, religion cannot be taught in schools and pupils must not wear religious clothing or symbolic jewelry. This has caused problems among the growing population of Muslims from France's former colonies in North Africa, who want girls to wear veils.

Traveling silk weavers

The Huguenots were French Protestants driven out of France by religious persecution in the 17th century. Silk weavers by trade, they used their skills to set up silk industries wherever they settled. In London, New York, and Virginia, their houses are recognized by large windows, which let in more light for weaving.

11

The Fabric of Society

French textile workers are highly skilled. Although these days local fabrics are threatened by cheap foreign imports, the fashion industry has always needed high-quality products. Top designers such as Christian Dior also revived traditional arts, employing peasant women for their skills in hand embroidery and bead sewing.

Wool and silk

The wool trade that began under the dukes of Burgundy (see page 6) now produces cloth for stylish tailored suits and outdoor coats. Tourcoing, Lille, and Arras, where the old merchants' houses can still be seen, are the center of the modern wool industry. By the 1800s, the city of Lyon was the European capital of silk weaving. Joseph Jacquard invented a special loom for weaving patterns into silk cloth. This speeded up production and allowed more unusual designs. Today Jacquard silks are used for coats and shawls.

The origin of denim

Denim is one of the most famous fabrics in the world. The name comes from *serge de Nîmes*, which means "workers' cloth made in the town of Nîmes" (in southern France). The cloth was dyed blue with indigo dye. Originally intended for rugged work clothes, denim is now high fashion.

Cotton prints

The cotton industry has produced two fabrics considered typically French. One, first produced in the 1800s, is called toile de Jouy. It has a repeat pattern of country scenes, such as elegant people enjoying a picnic, printed in a single color on a white background. Originally used for furnishing, it also became fashionable for women's dresses and children's wear. The other typical French fabric, produced in Provence, is based on printed cottons imported from India. These fabrics have small repeat patterns of flowers, fruit, and olives within a border. They are hand-printed from wooden blocks in bright colors such as yellow, blue, and pink.

Below: Provençal prints come in bright, bold colors, reflecting the hot sun of their native region.

Above: Toile de Jouy fabrics are usually printed in softer tones of pink, blue, or green.

Dressing with Pride

At one time, regional costume was looked down on because it was worn by peasants and servants. During the French Revolution, the government tried to ban it. However, country people soon went back to the costume that expressed their individual identity. Today they wear it proudly and are happy that tourists find it interesting.

Designs vary greatly between regions, but typical elements of women's dress are a full skirt and blouse, an apron, and a shawl. Caps, called coifs, and elaborate headdresses are always worn and matching collars with lace edging. In some regions, the headdresses have wide "wings." In others, they can tower up to two feet (61 centimeters) high and have to be tied under the chin with ribbons. Men wear white shirts, often embroidered, jackets, loose pants, and hats.

Two Breton women in full traditional costume, including intricate lace caps. No two caps are exactly alike.

Decorative details

Each region has its own style of embroidery and lacemaking, which is used on coifs and headdresses. The design, color, and decoration differ not just between regions but from one village to the next. There are important social distinctions. In Brittany, for example, married men wear a blue jacket, while single men wear a green vest. Young, single girls can wear a flowery shawl, married women wear a checked one, and widows wear a plain white one. The embroidery also tells a lot about the wearer. There are thousands of patterns, each indicating age and social status.

The world in miniature

At Christmas in Provence, people make Nativity sets of small figures called *santons*. These are clay models of ordinary peasants and workmen wearing regional costume and carrying the tools of their trade. They might include a farmer carrying a spade, a milkmaid with her milk pail, or a woman spinning wool.

These little *santon* dolls display remarkable detail. The sweets and glasses shown alongside them show how small they are.

Men in Vogue

French men like to look sharp, but they are not as influenced by haute couture (high fashion) as women are. Modern designers such as Jean Paul Gaultier have tried to persuade men to wear short pantsuits, bright colors, and even skirts. Most men, however, are content with attention to details rather than making major fashion statements.

Formal wear

For business and formal events, men usually wear a tailored suit made of fine wool, most likely in a shade of gray, blue, or black. Black and white is a traditional combination that is always popular. Designers such as Yves Saint Laurent have been supplying these clothes for decades. Silk ties add a touch of color.

Some young French men are brave enough to wear the pants or maybe the shirt from a new Paris fashion show, but not the whole outfit.

In summer, linen replaces wool. Suits and jackets come in shades of cream, beige, or gray. Younger men might wear a suit with a V-necked sweater under it or tailored pants with a polo shirt and a soft, black leather jacket.

Eating out

For a meal in a city restaurant or a night at the theater, a blazer or jacket and tie is expected. For Sunday lunch with the family or eating out in the country, most men would wear something like a cashmere sweater. A shirt with sweater tied over the shoulders is stylish but casual.

American influence

Like teenagers all over the world, young French men have adopted American fashion, especially jeans, sneakers, T-shirts with logos, and baseball caps.

The perfect shade of blue

Lanvin, the oldest of the Paris fashion houses, was opened in 1889 by Jeanne Lanvin. She was fond of a shade of blue seen in stained glass windows. She used this color so often that it became known as Lanvin Blue. Today most Frenchmen have at least one shirt in this shade.

Casual chic in a Paris sidewalk café. Waiters dress formally, while their customers relax in polo shirt and chinos.

Women Looking Their Best

French women are always stylish, even when they dress casually. They never look sloppy. *Chic* is the word usually used to describe them. It means they have natural good taste. Not many can afford real haute couture, but they buy carefully. A classic Chanel suit will last for years and can be updated with new accessories.

The Chanel suit is easily recognized by its trademark edging of tape or ribbon.

Comfortable in her clothes

Coco Chanel was the designer who established French "chic." She made clothes that were comfortable as well as fashionable. She was the first to use jersey fabric and the first to make pants for women. The "little black dress" and the cardigan-style jacket she introduced in the 1920s are still fashionable today.

Smart everyday wear is a tailored suit with a short skirt, a silk blouse or fine knitwear, and black tights. Younger women might prefer a stretch jersey top. For eating in a restaurant or Sunday lunch with the family, women will always be smartly dressed in suits or dresses. They wear high heels with almost everything.

A touch of class

For really special occasions, most women own at least one designer dress, but it will be simple and elegant. Extravagant details are considered tasteless. Younger women love the soft, flowing styles of modern designers such as Stella McCartney.

Color, fabric, and a perfect fit are more important than individual styles. Favorite fabrics are silk, cashmere, and soft wool. Leather skirts, jackets, and pants are also popular. Black is always the most popular color, although brown and navy are also considered classic. Cream and shades of beige are worn in summer, but bright colors are not common. For outdoor wear, fur is still popular, especially with older women.

Even quite young French women are happy to save their salaries to buy just one special dress.

Dressing for Work

The most distinctive item of a French uniform is the kepi (see panel). It is worn by the army, the police, customs officials, and other government employees.

French police, or gendarmes, wear light blue shirts and either navy pants or riding breeches and boots. Sometimes they wear a navy sweater with a stripe across the chest. For everyday duty, the kepi was considered inconvenient in cars and was recently replaced by an ordinary cap.

The classic kepi

The kepi is a high-crowned cap with a visor. It originated in military campaigns in Algeria in the 1830s. Because of its visor, soldiers called it the "duck bill." It was later adopted by soldiers in the American Civil War. During World War II, President Charles de Gaulle was always shown wearing a kepi.

There was an outcry in France when the government wanted to banish the traditional kepi.

Army and navy

Soldiers in the French army wear a beige dress uniform with braided kepis of various colors. The most famous branch of the army is the Foreign Legion, made up of foreign volunteers. Because of their distinctive headgear, they are known as the white kepis. Sailors wear red and blue. Instead of a kepi, they have a kind of beret with a stand-up band and a pom-pom on top.

The present-day French Foreign Legion wear sand-colored fatigues with distinctive red epaulettes.

Designer outfits

The French take their uniforms seriously. In 2002, they asked fashion designer Christian Lacroix to design new navy blue uniforms for Air France, the national airline. These included smart dresses and chic off-duty outfits. In 2007, Lacroix did the same for France's railroad workers.

Work wear

The unofficial "uniform" of manual laborers all over France is blue denim overalls. Farmworkers often wear shirts in madras check or, in Provence, locally produced printed cotton. French schools do not have uniforms, but many children wear smocks or aprons over their ordinary clothes.

Casual Clothing

In France, even casual clothing is chic. French women rarely go to the local store without putting on stylish clothes and makeup. Jogging suits and sneakers are hardly ever seen except on jogging paths.

In fashionable ski resorts, what you wear is as important as your skill on the slopes.

In fashionable resorts on the Mediterranean coast, the latest swimwear is on show. However, there is an unofficial dress code. Beachwear is considered very unsuitable in public places, especially restaurants and churches.

Sport for all

Riding bicycles is very popular. The annual Tour de France bicycle race inspires people to put on tight black Lycra cycling shorts and neon tops. Skiing in the Alps is another chance to show off one's fashion sense. Ski outfits with the latest microfiber technology and the season's newest colors are essential, with cashmere sweaters for "après-ski" wear. In summer, tennis replaces skiing as a social activity.

Another popular pastime is boules. This is played on a dirt surface with metal balls. The object is to land your ball closest to the marker ball. In villages all over the south, men in peaked cotton caps and short-sleeved shirts play for hours under the trees.

The French soccer team plays in blue shirts, white shorts, and red socks. The national rugby team also plays in blue. Both teams are often called simply "les Bleus" (the Blues). Replica shirts with the name of favorite players are popular with boys and men.

All over France, men enjoy a Sunday morning game of boules while their wives cook lunch.

Shocking swimwear

The bikini, a two-piece swimsuit, was introduced in 1946 by French designer Louis Réard. He named it after Bikini Atoll, the site of American nuclear tests carried out a few days earlier. He hoped it would be as explosive as the tests, and he was right. No model was brave enough to wear it!

Finishing Touches

French women are experts at adding stylish touches to an outfit. Every fashion house has a range of accessories, including bags, belts, shoes, and sunglasses. Even people who cannot afford the clothes can buy a small item to update last year's outfit.

A silk scarf knotted at the throat or a shawl thrown casually around the shoulders is enough. Women still wear hats for formal occasions and for going to church. Jewelry is always discreet. Most women own a single string of pearls, matching stud earrings, and a diamond ring with a simple setting.

Male accessories

Conservative French men show their originality by wearing colored silk ties and socks. Bow ties are not uncommon among older men. Other male accessories include leather belts and bags.

Even a casual country outing needs the correct shoes and handbag.

Men are quite happy to carry a purse attached to the wrist or on a shoulder strap.

Hairstyles

Long hair is not fashionable—for either sex. Women either have their hair cut very short in a "gamine" (tomboyish) style or pin up longer hair in a French twist. Older men still wear the typical mustache and pointy beard, but young men prefer to be clean-shaven or go for the "designer stubble" look.

Perfume

French women do not consider themselves completely dressed without perfume. The town of Grasse, in the south, is the perfume capital of the world. The Mediterranean climate is perfect for growing the flowers and aromatic herbs.

Although berets now come in fashionable bright colors, men rarely wear anything but black.

The beautiful beret

The famous black beret originated in the Basque region, along the border with Spain. It became a symbol of France when it was worn during World War II by the resistance fighters. The famous Alberto Korda photo of South American revolutionary Che Guevara wearing a beret, taken in 1960, strengthened this image. Berets are still worn in rural France and almost always by men.

Imports and Exports

International exhibitions held in Paris in the late 1800s brought together people from France's distant colonies. People saw traditional costumes and jewelry from Africa, Vietnam, Java, and Polynesia. There was a brief fashion of exotic styles.

Today North African immigrants have revived the 1960s fashion for caftans and ethnic jewelry. Designers have copied these styles in new, expensive fabrics. The fashion industry has also revived styles from France's past and sent them around the world. John Galliano, for example, has designed dresses like those worn by Marie Antoinette.

Dior shocks America

Christian Dior's 1947 "New Look" was very controversial. After the dull wartime fashions, it was refreshingly feminine, but the designs used huge amounts of fabric, which was considered wasteful. When he visited the United States, Dior ran into angry demonstrations of women. However, some were objecting because the longer dresses hid their legs!

The New Look featured cinched-in waists and full skirts. Dior thought it made women look like flowers.

France rules

French chic is the envy of women all over the world. Although they welcome occasional trends, the French feel their own style is superior. Older French people, however, like what they call *style anglais*. This includes the tweeds, corduroys, and knitwear worn by the English aristocracy.

In the 1950s, singer Juliette Greco and movie star Brigitte Bardot exported very different aspects of French style to America. Greco was a "beatnik." She wore black tights and black polo sweaters, let her long hair hang loose, and sang jazz. Bardot wore sexy gingham frocks and had wavy blond hair in a ponytail. In return, America gave grateful French teenagers Levi's jeans and T-shirts.

France's best export, however, remains the beret. No longer just black, berets are worn all over the world, in every possible color.

With her low necklines and peasant-style clothes, Brigitte Bardot was "every American man's dream of a French girl."

Glossary

après-ski Literally, "after skiing": the social aspect of winter sports.

beret A soft, round, brimless cap, usually made of felted wool.

boules A French game played with metal balls; also known as *pétanque*. The object is to place your ball closest to the marked ball and knock opponents' balls out of the way.

brocade A woven silk fabric with a highly decorative pattern.

caftan A long, collarless robe with wide sleeves worn in Africa and Asia.

cashmere A fine, soft wool obtained from goats, originally from Kashmir in India.

chic Elegant and stylish.

cockade A knot of ribbons, usually worn on a hat.

coif A small, close-fitting cap, usually worn under a headdress.

Corpus Christi A Christian feast day celebrating the Eucharist, or Holy Communion.

Empire style A simple style of the early 19th century; high-waisted dresses with flowing drapery.

farthingale A wire-framed petticoat worn to make the skirt stand out from the waist.

French Revolution A period of social and political upheaval in France, starting in 1789, that resulted in the transformation of the French state from an absolute monarchy to a government based on principles of democracy, equality, and human rights.

French twist A hairstyle in which the hair is swept up and pinned at the back: also called a French roll.

gamine Boyish.

gingham A cotton fabric with small checks.

haute couture High fashion.

Huguenot A French Protestant, especially in the 16th to 17th centuries.

Jacquard loom A mechanized weaving process, originally operated by punched cards, now computerized.

kepi A high-crowned cap with a visor.

linen A fine-woven fabric made from the flax plant.

madras check A checked cotton fabric originally produced in Madras (now Chennai), India.

Muslim A follower of Islam.

muslin A very fine, almost transparent cotton fabric.

New Look A style created by Christian Dior in 1947. It featured long, full skirts and nipped-in waists.

patriotic Proud of one's country.

Phrygian cap A soft, red, cone-shaped cap, originally worn by freed Roman slaves.

santon A clay model of a character from a Nativity set, popular in southern France.

Three Kings The Magi, or three wise men, who attended the birth of Jesus Christ.

toile de Jouy A decorative fabric featuring pictures of rustic scenes in a repeat pattern.

tricolor Literally, "three colors": the red, white, and blue of the French flag.

vestment Ceremonial clothing worn by priests.

Further Information

Books

Conboy, Fiona. *Welcome to My Country: France.* Gareth Stevens, 2000.

Ingham, Richard. *Nations of the World: France.* Raintree, 2004.

Mitchell, Alycen. *Cultures and Costumes: Symbols of Their Period: France.* Mason Crest, 2003.

Park, Ted. *Take Your Camera: France.* Raintree, 2003.

Tierney, Tim. *Louis XIV and His Court: Paper Dolls.* Dover, 2005.

Web sites

filetsbleus.free.fr/costume/coiffes.htm
Traditional costume in Brittany. In French but good pictures.

www.costumes.org/ethnic/1PAGES/ethnolnk.htm#Western
Links to sites with illustrations of traditional costume.

www.costumegallery.com/FrenchNat/
Regional peasant costume.

www.metmuseum.org/Works_of_Art/department.asp?dep=8
The Web site of the Costume Institute of the Metropolitan Museum in New York.